RELATIONSHIP
wrecks

A Dating Guide for Middle-Aged Men
(and the women who date them)

Kathryn Allen, DVM

Illustrated by
Tracy Hill and Mike Padian

Relationshipwrecks: A Dating Guide for Middle-Aged Men (and the women who date them)

Copyright © 2019 by Kathryn Allen, DVM

Published by Pachyderm Books
Printed in USA

ISBN: 978-0-578-52603-4 (paperback)
ISBN: 978-0-578-52604-1 (ebook)
LCCN: 2019907336

All rights reserved. This book or any portion thereof may not be reproduced or used in any manner whatsoever without the express written permission of the publisher, except for the use of brief quotations in a book review.

rev201901

Contents

1. Let's Get Started! 1
2. When It's Time to Meet for the First Time 38
3. Are You Ready for This? 52
4. Getting to Know You Beyond the First Date 61
5. A Little More on Intimacy 87
6. The Basic Etiquette of Making It Work 107
7. What Do We Want? 114
8. Breaking Up Is Hard to Do 134
9. Where Are They Now? 139
10. That's All I've Got! 143

About the Author 147

1

Let's Get Started!

Okay... I'll need to be careful how I do this. I think I want to start by saying that I absolutely, wholeheartedly love men. I would love nothing more than to be completely in love with a man who is completely in love with me and brings out the best in me, and I'd love to live the rest of our long and happy lives together. Although I have dated some truly wonderful men over the past fifteen years—many of whom I honestly thought might be "the one"—ultimately, they were not.

I have a theory about relationships. It's relatively easy to meet and enjoy the company of someone who shares common interests with you, and that's what the first three to six months of dating are about—sharing time and common interests. Somewhere between three and six months, however, the differences start showing up—not necessarily bad things (although there *have* been times . . .), just things that don't always work for each other. The challenge is finding the person whose idiosyncrasies match with yours. It's the truly wonderful yet ultimately wrong-for-me men who are my inspiration for this book.

Every tip in this book is something I have personally experienced or with which I have secondhand experience. By that, I mean some of the stories are from my most trusted confidants. More importantly, in most cases, it was not these things that led to the end of the relationship.

I have been so torn at times! Do I tell this man that he desperately needs a makeover, only to ultimately end the relationship anyway?

These are things that I genuinely believe someone needs to tell these men. Call it sisterly advice, but the circumstances of our relationships made it seem wrong to speak up.

One of the men I dated, the true inspiration for this book, is a special man. He's bright, engaging, and funny. He has a great job, great kids, and a great dog. He is genuine and sincere, and I wanted so badly for him to be the right man for me. Exactly why he was not "the one" is better left for my therapist (and possibly another book). Having said all that, on a more personal level, this guy was a disaster.

He completely lacked style in his dress, grooming, and home. He had put his personal life on hold while waiting for the perfect woman to sweep him off his feet. Even worse, he was a terrible kisser, which immediately had me worrying about our compatibility when things got even more intimate (and in this case, I was right to be concerned).

So here it all is in a book: things that I'm so flipping tired of experiencing in my romantic life. Come on, guys! Join the twenty-first century! Read a magazine or observe men your age on television or in the movies. Your years in middle age can be sexy too. Throw us a bone; make the effort! It may not ultimately change who you end up with, but I guarantee we'll all have a lot more fun getting there.

I'll Go First

I don't feel particularly different from any other single middle-aged woman in that as diverse as we all are, there seems to be (with most of us, anyway) a common thread and an unspoken understanding that we're all cut from the same fabric. That being said, we each have our stories to tell, and here's mine.

I divorced just after my fortieth birthday. We were living in Maryland, but my heart was in Arizona, so I packed up my two kids, the dog and cat, and a trampoline (thinking that would give my kids some feeling of consistency) and moved us to Phoenix.

I bought an older home sorely in need of improvements and immersed myself in its transformation. With the exception of moving walls, I pretty much did all the work myself.

I tore out carpeting, laid tile inside and bricks outside, painted walls, and planted trees. Home projects took up nearly all of my free time because I desperately wanted a comfortable, safe place that my children could call home. I didn't really date in those first few years, but I honestly never considered the possibility that I wouldn't find that perfect match for me.

Once my house was in reasonable shape and my kids got a bit older, I started dating. For those of you who think dating when you have young children is difficult, wait until they become teenagers. I was not prepared for the degree of challenges and heartache that followed. Ever optimistic, I have continued to persevere. I can safely say that I have given it my all. In fact, because my children are now adults and my most recent romantic hopeful had a fourteen-year-old and lived in Australia, I packed up my life and moved (along with three dogs and a cat) to Australia, hoping I had finally found "the one." The fact that he and I knew each other from veterinary school many years ago, gave me a false sense of security that I already knew him. I didn't.

We opened a veterinary hospital and tried to build a life together. It was an unforgettable two-year adventure (and possibly worthy of another book), but, alas, true love continues to elude me.

I love living in a comfortable environment. My house is small, but it's happy, and it defines me. In many ways, I love reading at Starbucks with a soy latte as much as traveling the world on an exotic adventure. I'm proud of the fact that even after thirty years of veterinary medicine, animals remain my passion. As ridiculous as I'm sure this sounds, the most emotionally rewarding part of my Australian adventure was the profound relationship I developed with an orphaned fruit bat named Kevin.

This book isn't intended to be hurtful or unkind. And even if it sounds jaded (perhaps it is a bit), I promise that its purpose is actually well intentioned. We all can use a little guidance, and I honestly believe that if men read this book and look beyond the humor (hopefully after having a good laugh), it might prove more useful than expected.

Grooming and Personal Hygiene

Obviously, the first step is to meet someone. If that first meeting sends her packing, you're not going to need the good advice in the rest of this book. So pay close attention!

There are lots of great ways to meet a woman, but most women require that you have a little something going on in order to clinch that second date. The exception to this is if you're lucky enough to have the opportunity to gradually get to know someone in a nondating environment, such as work or hanging out with mutual friends. In these cases, your first impression isn't nearly as important because we get a chance to get to know the real you in a nonthreatening situation. Sadly, the vast majority of us are going to be left with the traditional meet-and-greet scenarios. In these cases, your first impression really does make a difference. Let's review some of the more common and/or heinous mistakes many of you guys are making.

I know we're all getting older, and nothing (short of extensive plastic surgery) is going to make us look like we used to, but that's no reason to throw in the towel. We don't expect (or want) a man who looks twenty-five. If you're fifty, it's okay to look fifty. I don't know if you've noticed (probably not, since this book is directed toward men who have lost touch with the world around them), but there are some damn appealing fifty-year-olds out there, and we see them every day. When you were twenty-five, you may not have looked like Liam Hemsworth (the current version of Bradley Cooper in 2000 or, for those of you really out of touch, Frank Sinatra in the 1960s), and that was okay. You still did okay in the dating world, right?

So you don't look like George Clooney. Most of us don't expect (or want) you to, but that's no reason to stop taking care of yourself. You still have a long life ahead of you and a lot to offer, so act like it.

Let's start at the top and work our way down.

The Head Case

Bald is actually "in" these days, so why, gentlemen, are you trying to compensate for what's missing on top of your head with a ring of overgrown hair circling the lower half of your head? Do you remember Bozo the Clown?

Is that truly the look you're going for? Does the term "skullet" mean anything to you?

If not, it will. Read on.

We won't even dignify the comb-over with a mention here. Well, okay . . . maybe just a quick picture. Think about it, guys: Is this really the image you want us to have? If for no other reason, this could put a serious *damp*er on shower sex.

And on the flip side, to those of you with long hair, think again in terms of what you want in a woman. When you run your fingers through her hair, do you want to be running into knots and mats? Neither do we. I sometimes get the feeling that guys think the state of their hair doesn't really matter. Believe me when I tell you it *does* matter.

We don't like split ends, flyaway hair, or, even worse, hair that gets increasingly thinner with length so that by the time it's in a ponytail, the hair tie is holding only a few strands. If you don't have healthy, well-cared-for long hair, don't have long hair.

I should add here that an informal survey among women confirms what I have long suspected: many women find long hair unappealing. We think it substantially diminishes your masculinity. Ultimately, of course, you have to stay true to yourself. I'm just saying . . .

Worst of all (as promised), if you have both a bald head *and* a pony tail—actually, there's no excuse for this one. I think *skullet* is best defined with a picture, don't you?

Your Smile Says So Much

It's okay if your teeth are slightly crooked, especially if they're clean and white, but a dark-yellow snaggletooth is almost always going to be a deal-breaker. I think most women are fairly forgiving about less-than-perfect physical traits, but when it's something that's relatively easy to correct, then correct it! Appearances make a difference, gentlemen, and if you don't think you're worth caring for, what are we going to think?

Teeth are easily correctable.

There are all kinds of over-the-counter whitening strips, and these days, orthodontia is readily available at any age. There is no excuse for a large, protruding, yellow-orange tooth in your mouth.

Okay, I'll 'fess-up—this is one I know from personal experience: We met via the internet, and he seemed like a great guy, so when he smiled for the first time, I was genuinely disappointed. His tooth was so bad I wasn't sure I could overlook it long enough to get to know him, and I pride myself on not being overly superficial. In my defense, I did continue to date him. But believe me when I say that it took a few drinks before I had the courage to kiss him. I got past it but never stopped being embarrassed when my hair would get snagged in that damn tooth.

For the record, I get that it shouldn't be all about looks, and I honestly admired that this man didn't feel the need to fix his mouth. That being said, why take the chance of alienating someone before she even gets an opportunity to know you? Interestingly, this same guy confided in me that he would never date a woman who was overweight!

Back to Basics

This has been a recurring theme in my dating life, and to be honest, a hairy back doesn't bother me. I have a number of friends, however, who consider a hairy back an absolute deal-breaker. Guys, some of you have enough hair on your back to braid. From a hygiene point of view, it definitely holds in the sweat, which in turn collects dust and debris. From a sexual point of view, all that hair feels like a barrier between your skin and mine.

I've given this a lot of thought, and here's what it comes down to: would you date a woman with thick, hairy armpits or legs? How about a mustache on a woman? Well, many women feel the same way about your back. If you're okay with a "natural" woman, good for you! I feel fairly confident that she's going to be okay with your fuzzy nature as well. If, however, granola isn't your cereal of choice, you should definitely consider a little manscaping.

If all this sounds outrageous to you, you may want to sit down for what you're going to read next. I know more than a handful of women who feel exactly the same way about the chest, and below . . .

I think this may be a good time to remind my readers that this book simply provides some suggestions. What you do with them is, of course, entirely up to you. We're all different, and you need to stay true to yourself. If you have a strong emotional attachment to your chest hair, for goodness' sake keep it.

As I said, I happen to like fuzzy guys, but although I wouldn't dismiss a guy who is neatly shorn, plenty of women absolutely would send a wooly guy packing. It's something to think about anyway.

Available at Most Drugstores

Crest, Go Smile, Rembrandt, and many other companies make teeth-whitening products. Like almost everything else these days, they also can be ordered online and are available at most grocery stores.

Mangroomer (available at Target) will enable you to shave your back without assistance. Or, if you prefer, order the Razorba home back-hair removal tool at www.razorba.com.

Panasonic makes a nice nose and ear trimmer for about fifteen dollars. Mangroomer and many other companies make them as well.

Check out Amazon.com. Not only can you order all these items, but you also can get helpful user reviews so you can decide which product is best for you.

Can You Smell What I'm Stepping In?

I know a guy who actually tried to justify the bush of thick, dark hair seeping from his nostrils by explaining it was part of nature's natural defense to disease. Let's think about that one: do you really think older men need that extra hair because they're more susceptible to respiratory disease than older women? Babies? "Follicularly" challenged men? Do you feel the same way about all your original body parts? Your tonsils? Wisdom teeth? Foreskin?

If you're still not convinced, how about this: would you rather be protected from the occasional cold than ever having a chance of getting laid?

If your answer is yes, I recommend that you return this book. I have nothing more for you.

For the rest of you guys, you may want to take a good look at your ears while you're at it.

What's Your Personal Style?

Personal style is exactly that, and how you dress is a reflection of who you are. This is exactly how it should be. I don't want to change that, but there are some common mistakes that men in my age group routinely make. It's good to have your own style, but I feel pretty sure that most of you aren't striving for "middle-aged dork."

Do You Wear Short Shorts?

Gentlemen, a whole lot of you need to reevaluate the length of your shorts. Trust me, nothing ages you (and scares the general public) quite as effectively as a short pair of shorts on a middle-aged man.

With the possible exception of running a marathon, your shorts should not be significantly above the knee.

Now I'm not suggesting that you start wearing large-pocketed cargos that go halfway down your calf; in fact, I would strongly recommend you don't. If, however, the last time you bought shorts was circa 1988, it's time to go shopping.

Take a look around you, guys. Men are not wearing short shorts these days, and nothing puts you in the "old man" category quicker, except possibly if you wear black socks and sandals with those short shorts. Oh, and by the way . . . the same holds true for swimsuits (unless you're in a place more exotic than any of the fifty states).

You May Look Young, but What Are You Saying?

A few pointers to help the verbally challenged join the twenty-first century:

If you're saying:	Try saying:
Canteen	Water bottle
Marijuana	Weed
Thongs	Flip-flops
Underpants	Thongs
Rigmarole	Crap
Rubber	Condom
Booze	Alcohol

* Exceptions: If this book does so well that it actually makes its way to Australia, you have permission to say thongs instead of flip-flops, and men under fifty may, in some instances, wear relatively short shorts. I'm not saying you'll look good, but you won't be alone!

How High Is the Waistband on Your Jeans?

If you are a forty or fifty-something-year-old male, I do not recommend that the waistband of your jeans hug your butt cheeks, leaving your boxers to cover your crack, but we need to find a compromise. Please don't wear mom jeans—you know, those high-waisted jeans many moms thought were the best way to hide a belly that was once stretched to the limit. They don't work for moms, and I guarantee they won't work for you either.

This fashion decision becomes tragic when it's paired with a black belt and a snug-fitting tucked-in shirt.

Speaking of Tucked-in Shirts . . .

Of course, there are occasions when a tucked shirt is entirely appropriate (with a tuxedo, for example), but if you're hiking a mountain or running on a treadmill in gym shorts and a T-shirt, do not tuck in your shirt, and do not wear socks that come up to anywhere near your knees (or your calves).

Unless, of course, you want to look seventy-five years old and have all the thirtysomethings refer to you as "that adorable old guy."

The Art of Internet Dating

Let's face it: like it or not, the dating world is definitely moving toward the internet at lightning speed. I'm meeting more and more people who have found a life partner online. I know lots of people (me included) who have used internet dating sites and have plenty of horror stories to tell, but I still think it's a very useful tool that shouldn't be overlooked.

So how do you get that first meeting? What does a woman look for in a profile? More than you may realize. Women can be pretty detail-oriented, yet it seems that many men slap up a profile with little regard to the image it portrays. If you're serious about your profile, we're more likely to think you're serious about a relationship.

Be a Pro When Writing Your Profile

Ewww! Some profile facts are just wrong. Try to avoid words like *wet* and *sloppy* when describing things you like. Remember, women need an emotional attachment before they start thinking about intimacy, and those types of descriptions tend to bring on a visceral *ick* response. In fact, when talking about kisses, even the word *long* is probably a bad idea.

Actually, it's best to not describe any kind of intimacy preferences.

Try Not to Bomb with Your Photos

I'm sure you've heard the expression, "A picture is worth a thousand words." It's true! Don't just tell me that you like backpacking and travel; back the statement up with a full-body action shot. It makes a huge difference. Women are looking for more information than just your physical appearance in the pictures. Along the same line, we really don't want the topless close-up pictures. A picture of you in the distance, swimming in the ocean, is fine, but the close-up muscle-flexing shirtless picture will result in a lot of us hitting the delete button. That said, for goodness' sake post a few decent pictures. One blurred headshot doesn't do it for us.

I get that this is one of the many areas where men differ from women. Most men would be perfectly happy with one close-up bikini shot on a profile, but women are looking for much more. We're trying to decide, based on your profile, if we are emotionally compatible.

We want to know what you do for work and in your spare time. What does a typical week in your life look like? Do you travel a lot, go to the gym regularly, sail boats, love animals, hate animals, love reading on the hammock? Are you a night owl or an early bird? The more you tell us, the more interesting you become. We like men who are passionate about life. Use your photos as proof that you're passionate outside of the bedroom, and you're more likely to get us in the bedroom. That's just how we're wired.

So where are all the women, anyway?

I can happily and easily tell you where we are, but I'm going to guess that, for the most part, you're not going to like it. Here's the short list:

> Volunteering for animal rescue
> Wine tastings
> Healthy/vegetarian restaurants
> Chick flicks
> Coffee shops
> Yoga class
> Pilates class
> Spiritual events
> Inspirational/self-help seminars
> Bars that don't have sports playing on a big screen

Are you getting the idea? Trust me; we're out there in droves. We're just not in the places you want to be—and if you did want to be in those places, we probably wouldn't be interested in you.
Not fair, I know.
Here's the good news! There's always the internet, and it's really not as bad as you think.

Hunters on the Hunt?

On the same subject, I suspect there are plenty of women who are okay with hunters and are impressed by the macho hunter/provider thing. In fact, I imagine many women get turned on by the whole gun theme in general. Some of us, however, do not. Assuming your goal is to appeal to as many women as possible, it's probably best if you keep the pictures of dead Bambi off your site. Women who are okay with this are going to get the idea and still be impressed by the tromping-through-the-woods-with-gun-in-hand photos, while those of us who still cry every time Simba is presented to the African kingdom will be less likely to delete your profile. Think about your goal: Are you truly looking for a beer-drinking hunting partner? The same is true for sports. One or two shots of you at a sporting event holding a beer and wearing a football jersey are enough.

Actually, one is plenty.

Nobody Appreciates a Double Standard

Nothing is more irritating than a sixty-year-old man who is in search of a woman aged thirty-eight to forty-nine. Inevitably, they'll explain themselves by claiming to be a very youthful sixty-year-old. Okay, so does that mean this guy would consider dating a really youthful eighty-two-year-old? As a youthful fifty-seven-year-old, it really got under my skin that a sexagenarian wouldn't even consider dating me, much less someone ten to twelve years his senior.

And for the record, even if I did manage to squeeze into the age range of women he'd consider dating, if he didn't include women his own age, I'd be less inclined to go out with him on principle alone (sadly, I've had to get over that one or limit my dating pool to a group of about six).

So, guys, maybe you should include women up to your age (and older!) in your search. No one will force you to actually meet them, and you'll earn the respect of younger women who appreciate open-mindedness in a man.

You Do the Math

Let's say you're a very youthful sixty-year-old. Naturally, you figure that because you're so youthful, you should be with a woman fifteen or more years younger than you. Here's the problem: no youthful forty-five-year-old woman will be interested in a man fifteen years older. She's youthful, remember? Why would a youthful forty-five-year-old woman be any more interested in you at sixty than you are in a "youthful" seventy-five-year-old woman?

The only forty-five-year-old you're going to attract will be much less active or a gold-digger. Is that what you're looking for? Youthful people, male or female, want to be with youthful people.

The solution?
Date a youthful woman your own age!

Duh.
Thank you. I feel better.

Really?

Why do so many of you guys (and women too, I'm told) lie? Think about it. Would you rather show up at that first meeting and find your date is pleasantly surprised or sadly disappointed? To help ensure the initial meeting goes well, you might want to consider the following suggestions about describing your physical appearance. And for goodness' sake, think about what you're saying!

You're How Old?

Please don't lie about your age. If we're too shallow to consider a man your age, you don't want to waste your time anyway.

I think it's interesting that we all seem to think we look younger than our ages. The truth is, we all pretty much look our ages, and we all know what that looks like in another. So when you, a fifty-five-year-old, show up at Starbucks after claiming to be forty-nine, two things happen: we're disappointed, and we know you're a liar. Not a good start to a relationship. By the way, overuse of the photo editor to make you look younger or thinner is also a lie.

When Was the Last Time You Saw Your Abs?

If you are carrying thirty or more pounds of extra weight in your belly, you are not "athletic and toned." Stating that you are simply sets us up to be disappointed. To be honest, being athletic and toned is not an absolute requirement for me (or many women), but women immediately lose respect for a man who makes that claim when they learn that he's not even close.

Where Women Generally Are Not

    Sporting events
    Sports bars
    Hunting
    Fishing tournaments
    Boating and RV shows
    Car shows
    Auto-parts stores
    Logging competitions

I know what you're thinking: you've seen women at sporting events. Of course you have, but they were either with a guy, or they're gay (not always but usually). Occasionally, you'll see a group of women hoping to meet a guy, but your odds are way better at yoga class.

Did He Really Just Say That?

Okay, let's think it through, guys. A man once wrote "Must eat meat to meet" on his profile. I knew this guy personally and knew he was just trying to find a clever way to say he didn't want to date a vegetarian.

And finally, if you're stupid enough to write "I'm an animal lover; I love pussy," you deserve to die alone, sad, and penniless.

Yes, true story.

2

When It's Time to Meet for the First Time

So now you're looking good. Your nose hair is trimmed, you've finessed your internet dating profile, someone "swiped right," and you're ready for that first meeting.

Did you know that most people decide within the first couple of minutes whether or not they're interested in a second date? That's a lot of pressure (for both of us), and we could very possibly make the wrong decision based on an unfortunate initial blunder.

Too Much Information!

Again, I honestly believe it's very important to be yourself, but some facts could probably wait for the second or third meeting. We all have problems, and life is messy, but your first meeting is not the time to sort through all those issues. Keep it light and entertaining. Share your fun and interesting side! We're much more likely to care about your life challenges once we feel like we know (and like) you.

Is the Groupon App on Your Home Page?

Frugal can be a good thing, and if you're the kind of guy who knows how to get the most out of every dollar, good on you! This is a trait that will be admired by many women. Even I, who absolutely am not good at getting the most bang for my buck, very much appreciates and would probably benefit from a frugal man in my life.

Having said that, please don't use a coupon to help pay for our first dinner out together. I get that you're just being practical, but women aren't (as a rule) practical, and you'll just end up looking cheap.

Double Your Pleasure

By definition, internet dating (for many of us, anyway) means that you're dating more than one person at a time. I have no idea why this is so often the case, but like so many aspects of our lives, it seems to be feast or famine. If you're lucky enough to be in a particularly gluttonous dating period and decide to double dip in the Match.com pool, I highly recommend that you give yourself at least an hour of buffer time between dates. This is especially important if you have any interest at all in date number one. (If you don't, you shouldn't be out with her in the first place.)

If you decide to do the back-to-back meet-and-greet (and we've all done it), then for goodness' sake have your story ready ahead of time. That way you're not left at 6:00 p.m. on a Saturday night, an hour into a pleasant meeting with date number one, saying something like, "I have to go. I . . . uh, have this thing I need to do." With any luck, date number one be understanding, or date number two will be a better match. If not, you're pretty much screwed.

A better approach would be to tell your date before meeting her that, for example, you have to take your sister to the airport at 6:30 but really wanted the opportunity to meet, even if it was only for a quick cup of coffee. This is called a white lie, and it is perfectly acceptable in the early dating stages.

Don't Overdo It!

Easy on the gifts! As a rule, women love gifts. We generally are not, however, impressed with over-the-top gifts from someone we don't even know—or, more important, from someone who doesn't know us.

It makes us a little uncomfortable and makes you look desperate. Women don't like desperate men.

Once, on a first meeting, a guy gave me a ten-pound bar of gourmet chocolate worth $150 because I'd mentioned in my profile that I liked chocolate. It was too much, and I wasn't impressed.[*]

---

[*] I will, however, happily accept chocolate (or any gifts, for that matter) from readers who enjoy this book and want to show their gratitude.

It's Okay if You Don't Drink, But . . .

I once had a first meeting with a guy for happy hour at a Mexican restaurant. He was a recovering alcoholic, and I knew ahead of time that he wasn't a drinker. I didn't have a problem with that, and when we met, he was very nice. He needed a few pointers about style and a nose-hair trim but nothing horrible. We ordered nachos; I got a beer (at his insistence), and he ordered a virgin piña colada.

I'm sorry; call me shallow, but this one little lapse in judgment really changed the mood for me. He totally lost his sex appeal as I watched him sip that sprightly decorated frozen drink. I think it was the little umbrella that put me over the edge.

Are You Trying to Win Us Over or Scare Us Away?

Think about who you're dating, and try a little sensitivity. For example, if you're on a first date with a veterinarian, don't tell her a story about how you like to torture cats.

Yup, true story. This guy seemed so nice when I met him. We were both in a hotel bar at ten in the morning, watching Wimbledon. In case you're wondering, I was drinking orange juice, waiting for my car to be repaired just down the street. He had a sweet smile and wasn't overly pushy. (Respecting my space is a definite turn-on.) We had a brief conversation, during which I learned he was a photojournalist, and I told him I was a veterinarian. He told me he had a cat that needed vaccinations, and we arranged for the cat to be seen right before noon so that we could go to lunch afterward. In that hour we were together, I learned he had been to jail for harassing his ex-wife, his photojournalism "career" consisted of buying and selling sexually explicit photos of famous people for gossip magazines, and yes, that he enjoyed flinging his cat from his patio into the pool. Why, you might ask, did he enjoy this particular activity? He loved the fact that the cat always came back to him. Poor cat.

This was officially my worst first date ever, and to be honest, I was a bit scared. I had allowed him to drive me to the restaurant, and I was seriously concerned about getting back safely. Please don't think I'm putting this jerk in the same category as my intended reading audience. This man didn't have the ability to self-reflect, but I think the cat story was worth a mention because, for whatever reason, it's not uncommon for people to make fun of other people's passions. A sense of humor is an asset. Being funny at another's expense—not so much.

Things You Should Probably NOT Mention on a First Date

"My ex-wife had me arrested for harassment."

That one doesn't need further explanation, does it?

"I have a great business proposition I want to introduce to you."

No matter how great the opportunity, if you actually want a romantic relationship with a woman, the business proposition should be tabled. In fairness, I think this guy was genuinely interested in dating me, but he literally couldn't help himself. The conversation kept coming back to this great business deal he thought I might want to join. And yes, it was a pyramid scheme.

"Shall we split the bill?"

Touchy point, I know. Guys get the short end of the stick on this one, but I honestly think men should be fully prepared to pay on the first date. I'll even take it one step further: if we women offer to split the bill, don't accept. If sharing the cost of dating is an important issue with you, that's okay. Right or wrong, however, I think you should make that initial investment, and let your date contribute down the line, especially if the night went well, and you want a second date.

"My last girlfriend was in her twenties. I couldn't help myself. We had nothing in common, but her body sent me into a tailspin!"

Do you honestly think those of us in our forties, fifties, and above will be inclined to *ever* get naked in front of you with that admission hanging over our heads?

"My last girlfriend accused me of being gay."

Trust me. Once you put that out there, your sex appeal drops dramatically. Interestingly, most women will be infinitely more attracted to an openly gay man than a straight man mistaken for being gay. I think we are all more attracted to people who know exactly who they are; it exudes confidence.

"So...would you like to go out again?"

It comes down to this: don't ask the question if you're not prepared for the answer. Luckily, very few women are going to look you straight in the eye and say, "No, I don't want to see you again." We'll pretty much always say yes because nobody wants to be hurtful (although some will be). Wouldn't you rather get the news in an email when you have time to regroup and respond in the way you want, rather than go through the awkwardness of being told to your face?

I've been on both ends of this one, and absolutely 100 percent of the time, I did not want to have to deal with that embarrassment in person. So spare us both potential discomfort, and instead, follow up with a text or email. If you're not interested, just don't make contact at all. This is perfectly acceptable after initial internet-generated meetings.

Important Point

Just so you know, I was talking about first-date etiquette. No, gentlemen, I am not giving you free rein to cut and run in all situations (hopefully, this goes without saying). I'm talking about someone you just met—not a woman you've been seeing regularly for months, with whom you've dropped the "L-bomb" or been physically intimate. An entirely different set of rules apply to serious relationships. (When I have a little more experience in that department, perhaps I'll write another book.)

For now, let me just say that running away with your tail tucked between your legs is always a poor exit strategy, unless, of course, you are in fact a dog who is actually running away from his vet appointment to be neutered.

3

Are You Ready for This?

Now might be a good time to decide what you really want. If you're not ready for a fully committed intimate relationship, do us both a favor and don't pretend you are. Trust me; there are plenty of women out there who are just looking for a good time and a little companionship. There's no need to lead us on. If you're "just looking for one thing," find a woman who is looking for the same.

What Do You Really Want?

If her feet are too rough, her lip gloss is too sweet, her voice is too loud, her hair is too short, her house is too messy, you don't like her friends, and pointing out these imperfections upsets her, maybe she's not the right woman for you.

Oh, wait a minute... I need to flip that. Perhaps he's not the right guy for me! Clearly, men aren't the only ones who could use a little advice. I've learned from personal experience how these kinds of criticisms can affect my psyche. Throughout my dating years, I have received advice from numerous happily coupled friends. The advice that I get most often is, "Relationships are hard work," or "You're being too picky; nobody's perfect," and I have taken that advice to heart. I have changed my lip gloss, learned to whisper in the morning, apologized for rough feet, and panicked over the state of my house (which, in hindsight, was perfectly lovely and acceptable for company). I've tried to change my "tone" and not interrupt (I always thought I was interjecting, to show enthusiasm). I've needed to understand that many of these "negatives" were just me being me, and the people in my life who truly love me know and embrace this about me.

I accept that relationships can be hard, but if being with someone makes you feel worse about who you are, you need to move on—quickly! The longer you wait, the more it ultimately hurts you both. I've wasted too much time thinking I'm not good enough. I am, and so are you.

You're probably not ready for a committed relationship if . . .

You're not ready to delete the naked pictures of your last girlfriend from your computer.

Don't try to justify it by explaining that they're artistic and not at all sexual. All naked pictures of your past girlfriends are, by definition, sexual. The only exception to this is the picture that is shot straight between your ex's legs that has a baby's head emerging. And by the way, that picture needs to go as well.

You're thinking about the financial benefits or getting a little extra help around the house.

If the practical benefits of the relationship are more important to you than truly enjoying the relationship, there's a problem. Find a financial planner and hire a maid.

The idea that you may actually have to change your habits even the slightest bit makes you break out in hives.

You're incapable of at least smiling and acknowledging your partner when you've had a bad day.

I'm not asking for a dozen roses and a back massage, but a "Hey, baby, I've had a rough day and need a little alone time. Sorry to be such a grump. I love you," as you make your way to the bedroom, television, or garage would work wonders and very likely get *you* that back massage.

You have less than an hour a week to give to the relationship.

That's not a relationship; it's a booty call.

You're still surfing Tinder . . . "just in case."

It's Probably Best That You Have a Life Before You Decide to Share Your Life

I'm going to get a little philosophical with you now. Let me start by saying that, except for having read a couple of books by Wayne Dyer and Deepak Chopra, I have absolutely no expertise on the subject. This, however, has come up far more often than I would have expected, so here is my completely unprofessional opinion.

I think it's great when someone shows interest in my hobbies, and ultimately, I hope to find someone who embraces some of my passions and introduces me to his interests as well. Maybe I'm outside the bell curve on this one, but I get a little uncomfortable when someone I've just met jumps right in to investing significant time and money in my pursuits.

In Tennis, Love Means Nothing

I met a man who bought a new tennis racket, clothes, and shoes early into our relationship so that he could play tennis with me. I was a pretty good player, and he, basically, was not.

To be honest, I didn't really want to spend our early dates together chasing his balls. I would have much preferred that he use his energy getting to know me and giving me the opportunity to know him and his interests. Then, after some time together, it could be fun introducing him to tennis, and maybe he could open up the world of organic gardening or rugby to me.

The point is, we women are much more impressed with a man who is passionate about his own life and interests going into the relationship.

While I admire someone willing to try new things, this was a little too early, and he didn't really put his best foot forward.

A Step in Time Is Usually a Good Idea

Another man I dated loved to hike. Being from Arizona, I asked him if he had ever hiked the Grand Canyon. He replied that although he'd always wanted to hike the canyon or at least see it, so far he hadn't made the trip because his ex-wife had never wanted to go.

Well, he had been divorced for over ten years.

Do you get my point? I don't want to be responsible for someone else's happiness, and I don't want to be his sole source of entertainment. Why did he need a wife to go to the Grand Canyon?

People are so much more interesting if they already have a life to share. Maybe you have a fabulous list of exciting things you want to do, but if you're waiting for that perfect relationship to get started, right now you're just plain boring.

4

Getting to Know You Beyond the First Date

Just because you've decided you're ready for a genuine relationship doesn't mean you're out of the woods. Keep reading because there's still lots more to learn.

When Dating Becomes Competitive

It's pretty common to go on dates that are physically active, which gives me another great opportunity to point out how men and women are not the same. When climbing a mountain or playing tennis, showing off your athletic prowess by kicking our asses isn't, as a rule, going to impress us. In fact, many women find it concerning if you aren't able to quell that need to win when you're on a date. We tend to be much more impressed when a man shows genuine concern for us and is at least somewhat impressed with our physical efforts.

Basically, we want you to have a soft side . . . with us, anyway.

On a date, tennis can be a great sport for back-and-forth playfulness, unless you take it too seriously. When playing tennis with my boyfriend, he became so wrapped up in the competition you would have thought he had some serious money on the outcome (and no interest in me).

A couple of times he slammed the ball directly at me with everything he had, and when the score was tied at 6–6, 7–7, and 8–8, he refused my suggestions to quit and call it a tie. Finally, when, for the first time, he was up by a game instead of me, he suggested we quit, saying, "But we'll just call it a tie, okay, babe?"

He won the game but lost my respect.

You Pick It

If you say I can pick the restaurant, then let me pick the restaurant. If you have a strong opinion about where you want to go, tell me. It's so frustrating being told I can choose, and anywhere is fine, just to be shut down repeatedly.

Don't Set Yourself Up for Disaster

Many women are very physically fit, and I highly recommend that you don't assume that you can outperform your partner. When, early on in our relationship, my date suggested we hike a local mountain peak, I was excited; I love to hike, and he knew that I climbed that particular peak often. He said, "I'll give you a ten-minute head start because I need to get in a good workout."

There's so much wrong with that statement I don't even know where to start.

As if that hadn't been enough to raise my hackles, when we met in the parking lot (he was twenty minutes late), he saw a political bumper sticker on my car and immediately went into a diatribe about my obvious ignorance.

I don't really need to write a chapter on the futility of trying to change someone's opinion on politics (or religion!), do I?

As for the hiking, I didn't have any trouble keeping up with that man, which I very much enjoyed since he'd pissed me off on so many levels.

I Get That You're Just Trying to Be Funny, But . . .

I can safely say that most women don't enjoy playing "pull my finger." I realize that's probably enough said for most of you, but I can't resist; I need to interject another personal story here.

I have a son, who at the time was about fifteen years old. The man I was dating had, in my absence, played "pull my finger" with him and his friends. For days, I heard about the enormous, disgusting emission that resulted from the finger pull. They loved it.

So a few days later, when, in the middle of cooking dinner together, he stuck his finger out to me and asked me to pull it, I was disinclined. I didn't want to partake in this particular activity at all but especially not in his galley kitchen while preparing dinner. I didn't pull, he didn't cut loose, we had a romantic dinner, and I stayed the night. The next morning we had a full schedule—coffee with friends, a hike, a movie with our kids . . . and he woke up in a sour mood. He was angry with me, and I had no idea why. It turns out he was feeling bloated all night and felt he was unable to relieve himself since I had made it clear that flatulence was something I couldn't tolerate. So he had been up all night trying to "hold it in." Jeez.

Here's the point: I thought I was having an enjoyable evening with my boyfriend. I didn't have a hidden agenda when I chose not to partake in the "pull my finger" game. I really didn't give it much thought at all. Waking up the next morning to a man who was genuinely angry with me was a shock. Suddenly I had become the thoughtless, narcissistic girlfriend for causing him pain and distress all night, which kicked in my insecurity, and I started second-guessing myself. He profoundly misinterpreted something that, to me, was completely innocent. I should have walked right then, but I didn't. Why? Because "relationships are hard."

Okay, I get that we took a bit of a leap from stupid games to psycho boyfriends, and just because you enjoy games like "pull my finger" doesn't automatically put you into that category. And this guy was a lawyer!

I had a similar reaction from another man because I turned the lights off when I went to bed before him. He didn't talk to me for two days. No wonder I've learned to overthink things.

Are you starting to feel my pain?

By the way, once we're asleep, feel free to do what you need to do to relieve that bloated feeling. This does not, however, give you permission to hold our heads under the covers to experience the aftermath. Again, most (probably all) women agree — really not funny.

There's a Difference between Cyber Life and Reality

If you are asked how your day was and you respond by detailing the day's adventures of your Puzzler Pirates interactive internet character, we're not likely to be impressed. We really don't care how many shields you sold or blocks of gold you own. This is, however, a good way to impress our thirteen-year-old sons (kind of like playing "pull my finger").

Side note: The fact that your character has traveled across great seas and deserts is not proof that you love to travel.

Don't Compare Yourself to the Enemy

I once told a guy I'd been dating for a month or two a personal and honest account of why I thought my first marriage had failed and how I'd felt like I was never a priority in his life.

At the end of this heartfelt account, he responded very nonchalantly that my story sounded exactly like what he thought his ex-wife would say about him.

Did he really think comparing himself to the one man who exemplified what I hoped to avoid in my next relationship was a good idea?

Kudos to him for his honesty, I guess, but he was truly upset when our relationship didn't work out. Perhaps that was a time for silence and introspection on his part.

Do You Have a Home or a Shelter?

Eventually, the woman you've been dating will want to see where you live. Where and how a man lives tells a lot about his personality. Visiting a man's home has had a huge effect on how I've viewed him. I would even go so far as to say that some of the homes I've seen were, in fact, deal-breakers.

I dated a man whose home was such a disaster I referred to it as his shelter. It completely lacked the elements that, in my mind, make a house a home. His living room had a wooden-slat outdoor bench, a foosball table, and a tiny stand that held the computer. The Wi-Fi code was taped to the wall. His dining room had a metal high-top table and four matching white vinyl bar stools with black-and-red Harley-Davidson emblems.

Another man had a huge dining room with a cathedral ceiling. The room was completely empty except for a set of golf clubs, a tiny square of artificial grass with a tee, and a plastic golf ball—nothing else. Yup, he used his dining room as a driving range.

Now I'll admit it did cross my mind that if things worked out with either of these guys, at least I'd get some say on how we'd decorate our future home together. But these places were tough to visit. I couldn't help but question their taste, not just in decorating but possibly with women as well. Why would I want to be with a man who completely lacked discriminating taste?

Working from the Inside Out

Living rooms are not meant to be gyms, game rooms, or driving ranges. Dining rooms are not bars. Family rooms ideally should have enough furniture to seat the entire family at the same time. TV trays, I'm sorry to report, are not meant to be permanent living room décor.

Once, I did a veterinary house call for a single man in his mid-fifties who had expressed an interest in dating me. I walked into his living room and saw that he had two TV trays piled high with junk on either side of his La-Z-Boy, which was placed directly in front of his huge flat-screen TV. Almost every surface in the house was crowded with stuff.

Now, I get that there are times when you just want to sit back and enjoy the television while eating or drinking. I have totally had days where, along with the remote, the Chinese food and ice cream containers were within easy reach of the couch. *But* . . . I'm not going to leave that stuff there when I know a man is coming over—especially a man that I'm interested in dating!

In this particular case, it was obvious that the trays and their contents were not just happenstance. These trays had magazines, car keys, pill bottles, food containers, glasses, a cell phone, a lotion bottle—you get the idea.

At the very least, buy a couple of end tables with nice deep drawers and cram all your stuff in there when you know someone you'd like to impress is coming over.

For those of you who don't see the problem with this, here's my point: many women, including me, aren't looking for a relationship with someone who appears to do little more than sit in front of the television all day. Sure, most of us are guilty of that from time to time (in varying degrees), but we assume that in the beginning of a relationship, you're going to put your best foot forward.

If this is your best foot, we're concerned.

Somebody Call the Cops!

Another true story: I once dated a guy whose home was burglarized. When the police came, they observed that the burglars had ransacked the place.

They hadn't.

Try Not to Get Boxed In

Surprisingly, to me anyway, cardboard seems to be a popular furnishing choice among single men. I'm not sure why; perhaps it's related to the duct tape phenomenon. Another informal survey taken among my similarly aged friends revealed that more than a few of you find the set of three cardboard end tables with the faux-wood finish (widely available at most discount stores) to be quite the find. Others feel those end tables are a waste of money because a box can be easily flipped over to serve the same function. Either way, cardboard is being way overused.

And no, putting a tablecloth over the box does not fix the problem.

You're Not the Only One Dealing with Kids and Pets

If you have a dog, it's probably best if he doesn't own the furniture. It's hard to feel romantic when you get up from the couch to find your clothes have collected the dog's hair and slobber. I understand that many men don't make interior decorating a priority, but women want to know that you have some kind of control over your life.

These rooms—golf, clutter, foosball, dogs, cardboard—leave me questioning a man's ability to create a pleasant living environment and wondering about maturity levels. What does it say about a man who, in his fifties, chooses foosball or Wiffle golf over an environment conducive to the possibility of conversation, comfort, maybe a glass of wine, and a romp on the couch?

And please, don't blame the kids! Most of the women you'll date are likely to have raised (or are still raising) kids. We all know how much work that can be, and we get that they probably prefer a Ping-Pong table to a dining room table, but it's not their house! Come on, guys; regain a little control.

We don't have a video arcade in our living room. Why do you?

You Can't Judge a Book by Its Cover . . . or Can You?

Landscaping is a good thing. Like it or not, your home tells us a lot about you. If your idea of maintaining the outside of your house constitutes an hour of weed-whacking, you're probably lacking a little in the landscaping department. The outside of your house is the first thing we'll see on our initial visit to your home. It's just another form of the first impression. For most of us, it doesn't have to be a showplace, but it would be best if it didn't look like a crack house.

Are You Caught in the Stone Age?

The same holds true for the backyard. Two men I dated chose to wipe out the landscaping, opting for an easier-to-manage yard—no weed-whacking for them! The first guy took out all the plants and trees and replaced everything with stone, except for a small patch of grass in the middle (so his dog had a place to poop).

The second guy didn't even bother to provide his dog with a grassy patch. He made the entire yard stone; not a plant to be found. Poor dog, no wonder he was a hyperactive spaz that spent his entire day on the couch.

Guys! Your house is a reflection of you. If you're going to make your house a giant game room and your yard a dog toilet, we start to wonder who's in control. Many men may not notice these things, but most women do, and it makes a difference. If you have no control over your dog or your kids, we're inclined to have some sympathy for your ex-wife.

Don't Let It All Go to the Dogs!

Here's a little more about your dog. Before I start, let me just say that this section may not be a fair representation of what actually happens in the dating world. I'm sure that the fact I'm a veterinarian plays a role in a man's comfort level in exposing his pets to me. In fact, I truly hope that's the case because some of what I'm about to share is pretty dismal.

Focus!

Expose us to your passion in small doses. I realize that you have the most special dog in the universe, but maybe you should get to know a little something about your date first.

If you act like you're more interested in your dog (or anything you're passionate about) than you are in me, we've got a problem. I get that you (like me) think the world of your dog.

I also understand that—in the beginning, anyway—the dog probably does take priority over me, but you don't have to tell me that!

Sure, I'd love to see a picture, but the twenty-minute photo essay on a first date is a bit excessive. I'm using dogs as an example because that's been my experience, but obviously, the same is true for a myriad of passions.

Hunting and sporting events come immediately to mind, although we're probably not going to get overly excited about your car or coin collection either.

Yikes!

It gets worse. I've mentioned it before, but I think it deserves a repeat: when we come to your home for dinner or to watch a movie, we're on a date, and we've made an effort to look nice. I'm not the only one who's been to homes where there was no place to sit that didn't include a dog on the lap, a seat full of dog hair, or a couch soaking wet because the dog just got out of the pool and decided to take a nap. I may be the only one, however, who has been expected to sit on a couch that was soaking wet from the sticky rawhide the wet dog enjoyed while lounging after a swim in the pool.

I remember getting up from the couch, all wet and with dog hair glued to my skirt. As you can imagine, sticky dog drool and dog hair are not a very good combination. It's really hard to feel attractive under those circumstances, and when we women don't feel attractive, I promise you, we're not feeling very romantic either.

Here's Where It Gets Ugly

I soldiered through it with a smile on my face. I am, after all, a veterinarian. I actually liked this guy—what's a little hair and drool when we're talking about love, right?

But it got worse. The last thing a woman wants when that intimate moment arrives is a drooling, hyperactive ninety-pound goldendoodle joining in.

True story—and in hindsight, I blame myself for this one: I literally made love to a man for the first time while simultaneously holding off his overzealous hound—on my back, my right arm fully extended, grasping the collar of the panting, whining, drooling dog.

The. Entire. Time.

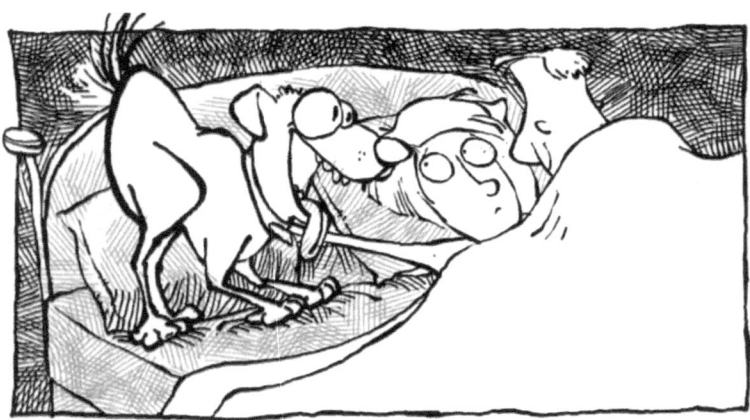

As I said, I blame myself. It's just that I'm a veterinarian, and everyone seems to think that this naturally makes me more tolerant of pets (and I think this last example confirms that assumption). In this particular case, however, I should have risked ruining the moment and spoken up. My poor judgment aside (and trust me; I could write an entire book on how poor judgment leads to disastrous romantic relationships), this particular dog did not belong in the bedroom.

Guys, I get that you love the idea of having a woman who fits into your life, one who enjoys the simple daily pleasures of cooking together, watching a movie, and relaxing at home. We want that too! But here's what goes through our heads — an automatic calculation goes on in the beginning of a relationship. We assume that you're on your best behavior and putting your best foot forward. So if you're a disorganized slob the first time we visit your home, we assume this is as good as it gets — well, I think you see the problem.

In our minds, a hairy couch covered with dog slime and sticky treats quickly turns into your dog's stinky, steaming dump in the middle of the dining room floor. Let's face it; in the beginning, you're courting us. We expect it. Make the effort — dazzle us! You may enjoy the result so much you'll find it's worth keeping up even after you've won us over. Trust me; you reap what you sow.

5

A Little More on Intimacy

Ultimately, intimacy is an area that's either going to work or it's not, and all the advice in the world can't change that. There are, however, some basic pointers that can make those special moments more rewarding for us both.

Are You Tied to Your Tongue?

This one has always puzzled me: How does someone get to middle age and still not know how to kiss? The more I think about it, the more concerned I get. Clearly, these men don't know how to kiss because no one has corrected them. Well, no one's ever corrected me either. Could it be that we all think we're great kissers, and most of us are wrong? Or maybe kissing is just a case of compatibility. I've decided that it's a little of both; when two similar kissers get together it can be fireworks, but sadly, the wrong kiss can seriously threaten a relationship.

Compatibility or not, consider this one important piece of advice: please don't lick your partner's face.

Tongues are a wonderful thing and a great asset when kissing, but there really is no reason for our tongues to come out of our mouths. Once out of the mouth, kissing becomes licking.

I don't particularly like it when my dog licks me across the face, and I certainly don't want you to follow suit. If I need a towel after kissing, we have a problem.

Underneath It All

News flash! Most women do notice what you're wearing under those jeans. And when that special moment finally arrives, going commando is not, as a rule, our personal preference. It is, however, overwhelmingly preferred to tighty-whities, especially if they're no longer tight . . . or white.

Sure, men are more visual than women, but we're not blind. Believe me when I tell you that when that magic moment arrives, it's going to be a lot better for both of us if you put a little thought into EVERYTHING you're wearing.

We will remember that first time for a very long time. Do you want those saggy off-white undies with the frayed elastic fringe to be the image of you we hold in our minds? Sadly, we women have plenty of pathetic briefs embedded in our memories.

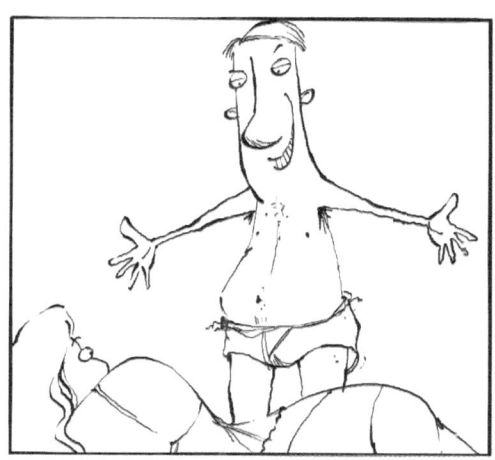

Hello?

There is a mandatory phone call (at least!) that must be made within twelve hours of having sex for the first time.

Exceptions to this rule are:

1. You haven't actually left each other yet. Duh.
2. Her husband came home and caught you in bed together.
3. You've had a medical emergency and are currently under anesthesia.
4. You're dead.

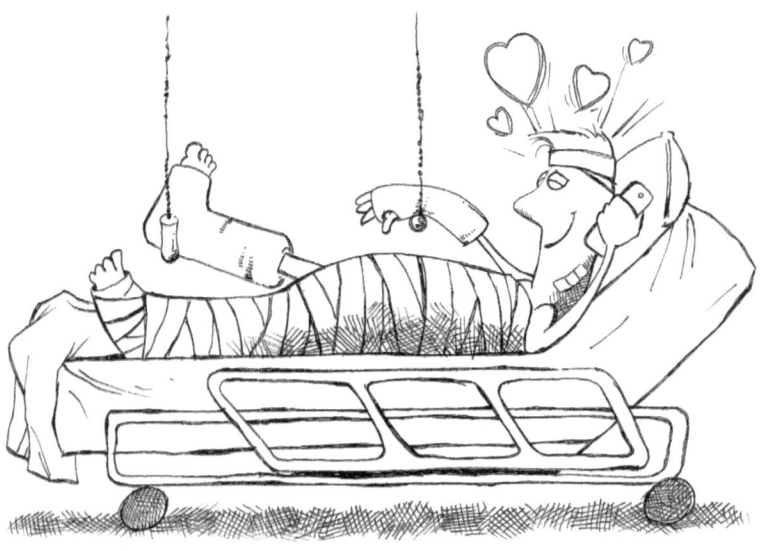

By the way, this holds true even if you realize that this is not the woman for you. Please, if at all possible, don't just disappear. I realize that on the opposite side of this issue is a very real message that many women (and some men) desperately need to learn: no message is, in fact, a very clear message. That said, there's a better way to handle these situations, especially once you've become physically intimate.

A Flick in Time Is Another Big Mistake

Okay, if you listen to nothing else I say, please listen to this. Do not ever, under any circumstances, "flick" with your tongue any body part of a woman unless your goal is to cause her extreme aggravation. I have to admit that this one has puzzled me for the longest time. Why on earth would a man think this is even remotely appealing or enticing?

Then I figured it out. A few years ago, I was channel-surfing, and I came across an HBO documentary on pornography, so naturally, I watched. There was a segment that showed the actors being directed on how to perfect the tongue-flicking technique! I'm not talking about a gentle, soft motion. I'm talking about an extended period of rapid tongue flicking that I imagine takes years of practice and training to perfect. I was shocked. Am I the only woman who can't stand this technique?

So I took a survey. I took a number of surveys! I spoke to women of all ages, sometimes anonymously, sometimes over a beer in a bar, and I did not find a single woman who enjoys this flicking technique. Then I rented a couple of porn movies (purely for research, of course) and wouldn't you know—my suspicion was correct. Tongue flicking is very popular in porn! Men (and women) are flicking tongues in ears, mouths, and . . . well, everywhere, and it appears as though the women on the receiving end are enjoying it.

So here's what some men need to understand: the women were *acting*. The sex in X-rated movies (or any movie, for that matter) is not real.

Trust me; I get how this happens. Many of us have fallen victim to engaging in bad behavior that seems so alluring in the movies. More than once, I have taken a shot of bourbon or a drag off a cigarette because it looked so comforting in a movie, only to find myself gagging or coughing. But if you attempt to please your partner by using this God-awful flicking technique, you're not only very likely causing extreme discomfort that borders on nausea, you risk revealing your porn-watching proclivity as well.

There's no illustration here; let's just move on.

Take Your Time

Men and women are different. We know this by now, right? When women shop, for example, we take our time. More often than not, I go shopping looking for one thing and return home with entirely different stuff. Men go into a store, head directly for what they want, buy it, and leave. That's great for you, but please don't approach sex the same way. In all fairness, this is an area where many men have improved greatly with age, but a few of you are still in way too much of a hurry.

Soft and slow works much better for most of us.

All Night Long?

For the record, I polled a lot of women on this next point, and although I openly admit we are not all in agreement, the overwhelming majority of middle-aged women don't care how long you can "last." Men are so proud of this ability, but I suspect they think this is way more important to us than it is.

In fact, most of us have had the unfortunate (and exhausting) experience of feeling like the sex was never going to end; not unlike the feeling you get while sleeping outside in the cold fully expecting the sun to rise momentarily, only to learn that it's 10:00 p.m.—not, I suspect, the effect you're going for.

Trust me when I tell you that we're way more interested in what you do with the time. This is clearly a quality-over-quantity issue.

Are You Popping Pills?

Many older men have benefitted greatly from the development of pharmaceuticals related to the bedroom, and many women are extremely grateful for this contribution from chemistry. I'm absolutely not suggesting that there's anything wrong with this type of medical intervention, but if your goal is to turn twenty minutes into three hours, you might want to consider leaving the pill in the bottle.

Please don't mistake sex for foreplay. The touching, feeling, and erotic playfulness that leads to sex could go on all night as far as most women (including me) are concerned!

Memo

Okay, I want to be careful how I say this. There's another problem that seems to be primarily (if not exclusively) the case with mature couples. For so many years, guys seemed to be anxious to just get laid, while most women spent their twenties and thirties having sex with men who gave very little regard to their partners' level of enjoyment.

This, thankfully, is almost never the case with more mature couples. I have found men to be extremely attentive to my needs.

Perhaps too attentive. How, you might wonder, can this be possible? Let me explain.

Women, like men, want to please their partners. Just because many women are capable of reaping the benefits of your affection multiple times a night doesn't mean we necessarily want the evening to be all about us. More than anything, we (like you) need to know that we're doing it right. Nothing excites us more than completely satisfying our partners. When you try too hard to be generous and make the evening all about us, it can lead to serious anxiety. We naturally assume we're doing something so wrong that you'd rather avoid that side of lovemaking altogether.

I suspect (and here's where I need to be careful) that this behavior may be partially due to some performance anxiety on your part. If you're one of the many (yes, many; there, it's out!) men who has difficulty finishing what you start, simply diverting all the attention to us is not the best solution.

You're not alone in this matter—trust me—and a much better solution is to be honest. If you let us know that it's not our fault and convince us that it doesn't affect your level of enjoyment, the outcome will be so much better for both of us.

Trying to cover it up by spending the entire evening attending to our needs is not the solution.

Can You Spell OCD?

If you can't make it from being hot and heavy on the couch to a good romp in the bedroom without stopping to put the wine glasses in the dishwasher, you should seriously consider counseling. It's called OCD. They have medication for that, and it's almost certainly affecting your love life (probably your entire life, for that matter).

Ready for Takeoff

Sadly, more times than I'd like to admit, I have been subjected to what many of you think is a talent particular to just you. I call it the "helicopter," but I'm sure other women have different names for this little demo. It's usually performed fresh out of the shower and involves full frontal nudity and a swinging motion of the hips, causing your most cherished body part to circle round and round, not unlike the blades of a helicopter.

Believe me when I tell you, we've all seen it before and it's not special.

A Little Side Note about You and Your Penis

Most heterosexual women like your penis, and we're certainly glad that you have one. During times of intimacy, I can safely say that we can be quite obsessed with it, but it is not (in most cases) your most attractive trait. Very few of us have a picture of it in our wallets or framed on our desks. So please don't wave it in our faces or slap the side of our legs with it, just to be funny. It really isn't funny, and we really don't like it.

In fact, as much as I know you don't want to hear this, we're much more turned on by your washing the dishes after dinner. Showing us your "special" tricks is kind of like us showing you our Maltipoo's sweater collection.

Bye-Bye, Baby

As I said, nothing is worse than the tongue flick, but there is a close second. Gentlemen, for God's sake, please do not speak to us in baby talk—*ever*.

Think about it! Is this really the image you want us to have of you? I don't care how safe and secure you feel in your relationship, I assure you it's not secure enough to survive this verbal blunder. Baby talk is never a good idea, but in intimate situations, it's just plain wrong. One good way to ensure that you never get laid again is to raise your voice a couple of octaves and start rhyming your words with a lisp.

Bordering on Repugnant

Once you've become intimate, one would think you'd managed to navigate your way through the many bumps in the rocky road to romance. There was a time when I actually believed that physical intimacy came hand in hand with commitment. I know better now and fully acknowledge that I may have been a little behind the curve on this one. I didn't realize there are a few things that we women should not assume, just because we've decided to take the relationship to the next level.

I have learned to take full responsibility in this matter, but just so you know, most women will assume the following once they choose to become sexually intimate:

1. *You're not currently in an intimate relationship with another woman.*

2. *You're not actively seeking a relationship with another woman.*

3. *You're not currently in a relationship or seeking a relationship with a man.*

4. *You're not married (silly me for not realizing that the top three could be true, and you might still be married).*

5. *You don't currently have a pregnant wife or girlfriend. (Again, shame on me for not asking.)*

If the list on the previous page is not the case when you become physically intimate with a woman, I can pretty much guarantee that you'll run into some trouble. Most of us will just disappear and lose (or gain) fifteen pounds, but you might want to keep a close eye on your valuables — you know what they say about a woman scorned!

In order to qualify as repugnant, there has to be some intent to deceive or cause pain, but this was pretty bad . . .

If you want a woman to take a little initiative in the bedroom, then I strongly advise that you show some kind of appreciation when she does. Otherwise, believe me when I tell you that she's never doing that again, and most likely you'll be back on the market.

A man I dated (and was pretty crazy about, by the way) was in bed, watching a *Seinfeld* rerun, when I "made my move." Now, I'm aware that many of you guys really love your *Seinfeld*, and for good reason, but come on! We've all seen these shows a billion times, but when I got playful, he just lay there. I could have been the dog sleeping at the foot of the bed for all the recognition I got.

He had the remote in one hand and was laughing out loud at an episode that he already had admitted to me he had seen so many times that he practically knew it by heart.

In this world of multiple reruns, Netflix, DVRs, DVDs, and YouTube, there's really no excuse for not giving me the attention I deserve, but that's not the point! Regardless of the wonders of modern technology, if you want the woman in your life to take a little initiative, then it's definitely going to be in your best interest to acknowledge her when she does.

I suppose it might have been more understandable if I had interrupted the final minutes of a live sporting event—okay, maybe even any part of a sporting event—but a rerun?

You can be sure I won't set myself up for that kind of humiliation again. Sadly, largely due to this incident, this particular guy and I are no longer together, and now he's known by my friends as the "*Seinfeld* guy."

Let's Take It Down a Notch

I'm happy to report that, although many of us have experienced truly reprehensible behavior, most bedroom blunders are on a much milder level. But this is where some of us have been before meeting you. Many of us will need some reassurance at this point in a relationship, and hopefully you now have a better understanding of why.

6

The Basic Etiquette of Making It Work

So you've met, she's seen the house, you got laid (hopefully without the dog joining in), and you really want this to work. Life is starting to look pretty good. This, in my experience, is when things start to get dicey.

There's obviously a definite attraction, and chemistry can go a long way toward keeping that attraction alive, but now it's time to get to know each other. I don't have a lot of advice at this point because I think it's important to be ourselves and let the chips fall where they may. There are, however, a few small pointers that may help things go smoother.

It Takes Two to Tango

For what it's worth, I totally realize that *I* am the primary reason I'm still single. Many of the men in this book have gone on to have fulfilling relationships with someone else. Why? Because they aren't with me. I can be a handful. I tend to be insecure, and I way overthink things. I have a special talent for taking small events and turning them into major problems. I try to hide my insecurity by acting playful and lighthearted, which in turn gives the false impression that I'm tough and can handle anything. I can't.

This is an important point because I'm not alone in this respect. I've come to believe that most problems between any two people start from some kind of insecurity. Some people lash out; others isolate themselves. I pretend it's all fun and games and write a book.

I understand that some of my issues were based on my tendency to overthink everything. If I could have learned to not take things so personally, I'd have had far fewer problems in my relationships. That said, ultimately, in relationships, *it is far easier to change a specific behavior than to change our emotional reaction to that behavior*. When feelings are hurt, it's visceral. When we feel insecure or rejected, all the logic in the world won't fix the situation, and pointing out why we're being illogical will only make matters worse.

The points I make in this book are, for the most part, pretty easy changes to make. It's not about being right or wrong; it's about wanting to make your partner feel safe and cared for because that should be your absolute priority. Dealing with insecurities is, quite simply, part of being in a relationship.

Times Have Changed

Once upon a time, there were a million reasons why we might miss your call. There were only two ways you could contact the girl you were interested in—go visit her, or call her on the phone (one that was firmly attached to a wall in her house). Calls were missed because we had to go to work, or the store, or the bathroom, for that matter. When we heard the phone ring but missed it, we had no way of knowing who it was. There was no caller ID or answering machine. You could easily get away with minimal or no effort in the calling department without upsetting the girl, giving you (I suspect) a little extra time to figure out exactly what you want.

Well, times have changed, my friend. We now have cell phones, call waiting, caller ID, Facebook, and email. There's really no excuse for not calling, and we know it. Trust me; you're not going to get the woman of your dreams if you're not attentive.

Repeat after me: "Attention, attention, attention."

Did I forget to mention that being out of town doesn't get you off the hook? Unless you're in a third-world country that doesn't have an internet café (and even that's unlikely these days), you're pretty much screwed if you don't keep in touch.

I suppose being in an Amazonian jungle could potentially be a legit excuse.

News Flash!

You're not more important than the woman you're currently dating. Or any of the women you dated before that. How do I know? Easy! You're not more important than anyone. Your job isn't more important, your opinion isn't more correct, your time isn't more valuable, and you don't suffer more when you're sick.

A very important and very busy man whom I dated (briefly) told me the problem he'd had in his dating past was that all the women were very insecure. Well, what did he expect? This man lacked the basic social skills of returning phone calls and being on time—always, of course, for a very good reason.

Here's my point: the only woman who will tolerate a man who behaves badly is someone who is insecure enough to actually believe that he is more important than she is and that she deserves to be treated badly. If that's what you want—great. Otherwise, you might want to treat the women in your life like they're every bit as important as you. Because they are, even the insecure ones.

Which brings me to another point . . .

You say you want a confident woman with high self-esteem, but do you really know what that means? Some men seem to hold the mistaken belief that it's the women with low self-esteem who are so needy. If they were more confident, they wouldn't feel the need to tell you what they want or complain when you're not on time. They wouldn't defend themselves when being criticized. Let's face it; they wouldn't be so damn demanding and needy, right?

Wrong.

Only a woman with low self-esteem will silently accept the hurtful things that men sometimes say or do (often unintentionally, I admit) in a relationship. Relationships are tough, and they take a lot of open-mindedness and hard work. If, every time a woman expresses concern or disappointment in the relationship, you respond by getting angry or assuming she is too insecure and needy, you're missing the boat, my friend. An insecure woman won't think she has a right to speak up and express her feelings. A confident woman knows what she needs and deserves and will work at trying to make that happen.

So give it some thought. Do you really want a confident, capable woman? Or are you more interested in someone who will quietly go along with you and not challenge you? There's no right answer here, but if you're looking for a Stepford wife, you may want to consider a mail-order bride from Russia.

7

What Do We Want?

Women are confusing. They say one thing and mean another. They're impossible to please. Each woman is a mystery.

I must admit that many of these statements seem to be true for a lot of women. Not all women (or men, for that matter) are alike, but there is one thing that I have found to be nearly universal among women: what women really, really want is attention.

Let me explain:

WE WANT ATTENTION

We want your attention. We want you to call or text us. We want you to remind us how much you care about us. We want you to give us flowers. We don't want you to stop reminding us how much you care about us. We want notes left on our cars in the morning. Okay, maybe not after we've been married twenty-five years—*wrong*! You didn't fall for that one, did you? Even after twenty-five years, *especially* after twenty-five years. (I realize I'm getting ahead of myself here.)

Attention. It's what's going to continue to get you laid. What we really, really want is attention. So read carefully because there will be a quiz at the end of this section. The question will be, "What do women really want?"; the answer will be, *"Attention!"*

Okay, I know many of you are saying to yourselves, "But I did that!" You were crazy about her; you called her all the time and thought about her all day. You fell hard and weren't afraid to show it—only to have your heart broken.

What happened?

Can I be blunt? Attention only works when it comes from the right person. If she likes picnics and you're taking her to five-star restaurants, maybe you're with the wrong woman.

Women are tough. We know the difference between habitual attention and genuine gestures. If you're with the wrong woman, it probably won't feel genuine to her. Making the effort and having it not work hurts. Trust me; I've experienced gut-wrenching, ego-crushing rejection plenty of times and have the size-two jeans (thankfully, they're in storage at the moment) to show for it.

Here's the problem: you tried being attentive,

and it bit you in the ass. So now you've decided that you're not going to set yourself up for that kind of hurt again. Could you possibly be messing up with your soul mate? (Are you getting this, TN? I know you know who you are!)

So how about this? Keep being attentive, get knocked down, and get back up again and again. If I'm still standing (and I am), so can you.

Did I mention that women want attention?

*

---

*Answer: Attention!

More on Attention

Guys, I know you think I'm beating a dead horse (something, as a veternarian and animal lover I would *never* do) but I feel reasonably sure that most of you still have no idea how important this is to us. So I'm going to share a story about sticky notes.

I was explaining to a male friend how important attention is to women. He told me how he finally learned that one the hard way. He was in a relationship with a woman for a couple of years, and in the beginning, he would leave her little notes around, with drawings of the two of them, for her to find. (I totally melted when he told me this.)

As the relationship progressed, the frequency and number of notes steadily declined, and she kept asking what was wrong.

In her mind, his feelings for her had diminished. He still left her the occasional note, which he thought should be enough. I think you guys feel like the fact that you're with us (and having sex) should be proof enough that you're into us. Believe me when I tell you: it's not. He admits that she kept reminding him how important attention was to her, but he never really got it until after the relationship ended.

I think the next woman to cross his path will get a lot of sticky notes with drawings on them, and what do you want to bet they'll live happily ever after?

We Both Only Have One Thing on Our Minds

I've given this a lot of thought, and I'm pretty sure that attention for women is very much like sex for men. We want it all the time, and you really can't give us too much of it.

And I'm sorry to report that for women, sex doesn't count as attention.

Telling us how much you love us during sex also doesn't count. We need our attention independent of the sex. That doesn't mean we don't like sex; most of us like sex very much.

I'm about to give you some very important information, so listen up. For men, sex is the way they emotionally connect to their partners (so I'm told, anyway).

This is *not* the case for women, no matter how wonderful the sex. If you've had a misunderstanding with your partner, make-up sex does not set things right. A loving text message, a sticky note on the bathroom mirror, a flower on the windshield, or all three—these are the things that will make us overlook a myriad of flaws.

Here's a little rule of thumb: as often as you think about sex, that's how often we want attention.

Don't panic; you're probably not getting sex as often as you think about it, and most women realize that we can't expect attention as often as we think of it, but it's something to consider.

    I find it interesting that men often pride themselves on understanding a woman's needs in the bedroom, and knowing how to please her is something worthy of significant effort.

    Our needs outside the bedroom, however, are every bit as important to us—more, actually. A happy, successful, self-confident woman will not be content in a relationship that doesn't include some sensitivity outside the bedroom.

Attention Isn't Just an Action Verb. Are You Listening?

We really like you to listen to us, and most of us can figure it out pretty quickly when you're not really listening. You might think you're getting away with only partly paying attention, but you're probably not. Most likely, it will catch up with you at some point because women are like elephants: we don't forget.

Take gift giving, for example. It's very hard to tell a man (or anyone, for that matter) that a particular gift is not what we wanted, a disappointment. So we get caught in the rut of sounding appreciative for politeness sake, which unfortunately tends to exacerbate the situation.

Here's my point: if I tell you on Monday that I look terrible in hats and never wear them, don't give me one on Thursday. Just because I thanked you for it does not mean that I actually liked it. If I never wear it, and you're paying attention, you won't give me another one (I hope) at the next gift-giving opportunity.

Ho-Ho-Ho

Years ago, when I was married, my husband gave me a pair of sweatpants for Christmas. I didn't like them, and I didn't want them, but it was Christmas, so I thanked him and told him that I loved them. I never wore them, however, and by about February, he started wearing them.

The next Christmas, I got another pair of sweats from him. Again, it was Christmas so I was polite, thanked him, told him I loved them, and then never wore them.

Now, I would think, if he were paying attention, that he would start to figure out that I didn't want sweatpants as a gift, but damned if I didn't keep getting them for years to follow. All I can figure is that he was hell-bent on finding me a pair that I liked. Meanwhile, I felt invisible.

When Listening Is Painful

Please, guys, let us tell our stories our way. I know this can sometimes be painful. I know that you could probably do a much better job at telling the same story, and do it in sixty or fewer words. The problem is that when you cut us off and/or try to bottom-line the story for us, it takes the wind right out of our sails.

I will tell you straight up—you're right. Women are much more verbal than men, and we need some time to say what we want to say in the way we want to say it. You're right. You could get the same story said in half the time, but cutting us off and not letting us finish is really hurtful, and we no longer feel special.

If you're a heterosexual man who wants to be in a relationship with a woman, then you should want her to feel cherished. Chances are she will be very verbal. The way I see it, you have two choices on this one. You can be right and alone, or you can hunker down and listen to her story.

For the record, we know the difference between pretending to listen and actually listening. An occasional comment relevant to what we're saying can make all the difference.

You know, occasionally we can be quite interesting.

The Art of Gift Giving

I can only imagine how frightening it must be for a man to find the right gift for a woman. Every little decision is analyzed, picked apart, and then reanalyzed. To most men, it must seem ridiculous, and quite honestly, as I read my own words, I find myself agreeing. It is crazy.

But when my husband handed me my third pair of sweats for the third Christmas in a row, somehow all logic and reason left me. I was hurt and dumbfounded. What was he thinking? All I can figure is that his need to succeed in giving me the perfect pair of sweats far outweighed his desire to really please me. From a female's point of view, that can be deeply hurtful.

In the world of gift giving, women are a lot more difficult than men. A man will tell us what he wants and be happy when that's exactly what he gets. It can come early or late, wrapped or unwrapped; he doesn't care. If it's the wrong size or style, no problem; he'll simply return it for what he wants. He won't consider it a sign that his wife isn't really listening or that she didn't care enough to get it right.

Hell, he'll even go out and buy it himself *and* pay for it. He's just psyched he got his gift!

For Women, Every Gift Has Meaning

With women, every step of the gift-giving process is a sign and has a meaning. If the gift is late, we're just an afterthought. If it's not wrapped, we're an obligation, just one more thing on the to-do list. Wrong size, color, style, or make? You're not listening to us, and you don't care enough to learn these things.

Actually, it's even worse than that; you don't care enough to *want* to learn every little thing about us.

Are you giving us the same thing every year? Yikes!

Read on, and I'll gladly explain the error of your ways from a woman's point of view.

First Degree Murder Is a Much Bigger Deal

There's an art to gift giving. We want to feel special. A really wonderful gift is one that makes us feel special, regardless of its value. That means there can be nothing about the gift that implies a last-minute rush. When we get a nicely wrapped gift, we know that you didn't just buy it twenty-seven seconds ago on your way home from work. If this gift took obvious planning (like a trip, and you've already purchased the tickets and made hotel reservations), then we know there was some premeditated thought. Talk about attention! Boy, there are some real bonus points for that! There's a reason why first-degree (premeditated) murder holds a much harsher punishment than second-degree murder—planning ahead of time is a much bigger deal.

We're Really Not Interested in Practicality

I once got a birthday gift from a guy, handed to me when he came home from work. It was still in the store bag, along with the receipt and the unsigned card.

When I pointed out that he forgot to sign my card, he explained that he'd done that intentionally to allow for—get this!—re-carding.

Another man gave me a necklace for my birthday. It was perfectly nice, but when he let it slip that he had purchased it years ago (long before we had ever met), I was disappointed. See, he just let me know that it was most likely something he pulled off his shelf at the last minute and perhaps was a gift originally purchased for someone else, rather than something he bought with me in mind.

Guys, I get that if a particular gift is something you really wanted, it's unlikely that you will give a damn how it comes to you. But to most of us women, it matters.

First degree is a bigger deal than second degree.

The Importance of a Proper Apology (It's Really Important)

Whoever said "Love is never having to say you're sorry" was full of crap. We are all loving, feeling, emotional beings, and we're flawed. So let's start by acknowledging that we *all* occasionally will make mistakes in the relationship. When that happens, *apologize*! And for the record, a quick "sorry" said under your breath is not an apology, unless you're a four-year-old who just spilled his juice on the carpet.

> **A proper apology has four mandatory parts:**
> 1. Being able to explain what you did wrong.
> 2. Acknowledging how that made your partner feel.
> 3. Showing genuine remorse for what you did.
> 4. Promising to sincerely try not to do it again.

Working through problems effectively is where our communication skills are truly put to the test. Ideally, our differences help us understand each other and to grow together as a couple. Telling your partner to *relax*, followed by a quick *sorry* under your breath, however, will not end well. Ever.

By the way, it is possible to say or do something that's totally justified but it can still be upsetting or hurtful to another. Telling someone you're sorry to have upset her doesn't automatically mean that you were wrong. If you love someone and she is hurt, that should matter to you. Telling her that you're sorry to have upset her can make all the difference in stressful situations. Quite honestly, if that isn't how you feel, then you shouldn't be in a relationship with her in the first place.

8

Breaking Up Is Hard to Do

I think it goes without saying that anyone who's dated as much as I have has broken up a number of times as well. I realize that this book is intended to be dating advice, and hopefully you will find relationship bliss in a much timelier fashion than I have, but let's be real here. Some of you are going to break up at least once or twice.

I'm able to justify this section because how you handled your past breakup can definitely affect your next relationship.

Do You Know Who Your Friends Are?

After a breakup, most women don't want to be your friend. I'd say the likelihood of our remaining friends is inversely proportional to the intensity of the relationship.

You may think you're still friends with your exes, but more than likely you are not. The general consensus among all the women I've talked to is this: we're pretty sure the ex-girlfriends you think you're friends with are actually hoping for more and going along with the "just friends" thing because they don't want to lose you. You may not realize it, but we do. Every single woman I polled on this subject said the same thing; she is *not* friends with any of her exes. I'm not exaggerating—every single one.

Yet most of the men I've dated claim that they're still friends with the women of their pasts. You do the math.

Even more irritating is the air these men have when they tell me about their friendships with past girlfriends. It's as if it proves what great guys they are, when actually all it proves is how oblivious they are.

Friends or Friendly?

There's a big difference between being *friends* and being *friendly*. I'm still friendly with many men from my past.

This is called "being civil."

Your exes are not your best friends, and no woman should have to tolerate someone who was once physically intimate and passionate with you being in your life on an emotionally intimate level. If you can't move on, you shouldn't be in a committed relationship.

Which kind of brings us back to those naked pictures. Hmm . . .

A Day Late and a Dollar Short

Why is it that once a relationship ends, you suddenly become the caring, attentive man who was missing from the relationship?

A guy I dated seemed to have completely checked out of the relationship. Everything was about him, despite the fact that I was going through a particularly stressful time, had a lot on my plate, and definitely could have used a little help. Things got so bad (remember the *Seinfeld* rerun story?) that I finally pulled the plug, at which point I got the "How can I help?" post-breakup letter.

If you really want to do the "kind" thing, remain the jerk you were when we broke up; then at least you're not messing with our emotions and causing even more pain.

"I do hope we can remain friends and I'd love to take you to the airport, fill your prescription or anything else I could do to help."

Don't Look Back

As tough as this is to say, once you break up, you should probably remain broken up, although I'll admit there are exceptions.

This is advice that I need as much as anyone. It's so easy to remember the good times when you're alone and lonely, but don't second-guess it. You broke up for a reason, and it's time to move on.

9

Where Are They Now?

I've lost touch with many of the men I've written about in this book, and there are others I truly wish would just disappear, but I keep in touch with a few of them on a fairly regular basis, usually when they bring their pets in for veterinary care. (I even implemented a sliding-scale discount system for my exes who are still clients.)

Of the men I'm still in contact with, I am happy to report that many of them are either married or in long-term relationships, including the "pull my finger" guy. I guess it just goes to show there's someone for everybody.

It also confirms what I stated in the beginning of this book: most of what's in here are not deal-breakers, just some helpful (hopefully) advice.

As for me . . . this book has been a work in progress for a few years. As you might suspect, my dating status (and commitment to writing) has waxed and waned significantly during this time. I have written my personal update multiple times, only to find it needed rewriting by the next time I found myself editing this page. I've been extremely happy and fulfilled as a single woman, but remain forever optimistic that it's possible to find true love.

So if you will permit me one last personal story . . .

As you know, I followed a man to Australia. This man wasn't perfect, of course, but my God, was he attentive. When I walked into the room, his face lit up. When I spoke, it was as if droplets of gold were falling from my mouth. No one had ever made me feel so special, and it was intoxicating. So I sold my business and most of my personal belongings, left the house that I had turned into my sanctuary, shipped three dogs and cat, and started my new life on the other side of the world.

The minute I moved into his house everything changed—the attention, the admiration, the excitement. It was like someone flipped a switch. I know what you're thinking: what did I expect? That type of intensity doesn't last, and to expect it is unrealistic. Fair enough, but is it really that hard to treat your partner like she's your everything—a touch on the shoulder, a smile when she walks up to you, supporting her point of view on issues? (By the way, this advice applies to women as well.) We want someone who makes us feel safe to be exactly who we are, knowing that (for you, anyway) we're good enough just being ourselves.

Maybe that's why Kevin (the orphaned fruit bat I raised) meant so much to me. That little guy chirped and flapped his wings every time I entered his room. Once he learned to fly, I had a hard time keeping him off me—not just when I came in with food but every time he saw me. The truth is, by the time Kevin entered my life, I was pretty starved for attention. Lots of issues led to my return from Australia, but ultimately, it all came back to attention.

It just shouldn't be that hard, especially when the reward is so great. Just because the excitement of the dating period has passed doesn't mean you can't continue to be her biggest fan, always have her back, and keep her your priority. If I'd had that, I'd still be in Australia.

Love is, after all, what it's all about.

Veterinary Hospital Discount Policy for Dr. Allen's Boyfriends

Relationship Status	Discount
Dating before intimacy	30%
Exclusive intimate relationship	100%
First six months after breakup	50%
Six to twelve months after breakup	20%
Twelve-plus months after breakup	0%

10

That's All I've Got!

So there you have it: a collection of tidbits on relationships (and their wreckage) that I've accumulated over the years. It began with my telling these stories as they occurred, usually to my work colleagues or at happy hour with my friends. The stories were so well received that I started writing them down, and after a while, it became cathartic for me. I hope they made you laugh and possibly even inspired a few of you to rethink some of your choices.

To the men of my past, some of whom will undoubtedly recognize themselves, I just want to say thank you. Thank you for some great memories and even better stories. I have no regrets, and hopefully you don't either.

And to those men of my past who are wondering whether or not they're in this book, let me just say this: Absolutely not. You're the only one who didn't make it in.

About the Author

Kathryn Allen was born in Phoenix, Arizona, and has lived there most of her life. Hiking the Arizona mountains, exploring every corner of her beloved state, is where her heart has always been. Her passion, however, doesn't stop in Arizona. She has been to every continent except Antarctica (still on the bucket list). She worked with elephants in Thailand, taught English in Tanzania, swam with humpbacks in Tonga, hiked the Andes in Peru, and much more. She has a journalism degree from the University of Arizona and a veterinary degree from Cornell University. She has raised two children and is currently working as a small-animal veterinarian in Phoenix, where she lives with two dogs and a cat.

For more information about this book, please see www.relationshipwrecks.com.

www.ingramcontent.com/pod-product-compliance
Lightning Source LLC
Chambersburg PA
CBHW021953290426
44108CB00012B/1055